ANIMAL STORIES
HADROSAUR'S QUEST
A DINOSAUR ADVENTURE BOOK

HADROSAUR'S QUEST

By Brad Fossil

Creative Editor: Christian Darkin

> Copyright 2024 By Christian Darkin
> All rights reserved. This book or any portion thereof may not be reproduced or used in any manner whatsoever without the express written permission of the publisher except for the use of brief quotations in a book

Contents

Contents 3
Chapter 1 5
Chapter 2 13
Chapter 3 17
Chapter 4 23
Chapter 5 29
Chapter 6 33
Chapter 7 37
Chapter 8 43
Chapter 9 47
Chapter 10 51
Chapter 11 53
Chapter 12 59
Chapter 13 63
Chapter 14 67
Chapter 15 71

Cresta's World 75
Other Animal Stories 83
T.Rex's Battle: Chapter 1 87

Chapter 1

Dinosaur Provincial Park, Canada. 75 Million Years Ago...

As the first light of dawn stretched across the sky, it painted the vast plain in warm oranges and pinks. The early morning sun peeked over the horizon, casting a golden glow that made the dew on the leaves shimmer like tiny jewels. Far off in the distance, the deep, resonant roar of a waking dinosaur rumbled through the air, a morning call that echoed across the ancient landscape.

Near the winding rivers, life was stirring. The waterways, broad and filled with the night's rainfall, bustled with activity. Fish darted beneath the surface, sending ripples across the water, while amphibians croaked their throaty songs from the muddy banks. The sound of the flowing water was joined by the calls of creatures greeting the new day.

In the thick underbrush, there was movement. Small mammals scurried between the shadows, and insects buzzed as they took to the air. The rising sun filtered through the canopy, creating a dance of light and shadow that played across the forest floor.

And there was Cresta. The young Corythosaurus stood out with his vibrant crest, which caught the first rays of the sun and glowed with hues of red and orange. His body was agile, built for navigating the dense vegetation of his home. The scales covering his skin had a rough texture, and they glistened with a mix of greens and browns that camouflaged him well in the dappled sunlight.

Cresta was busy looking for his breakfast, his sharp beak nipping at the tender leaves of low-hanging branches.

He moved with careful steps, his still-growing limbs not quite as steady as those of the older herd members. He took a bite and savoured the fresh taste of the vegetation, his keen eyes scanning the surroundings for any signs of danger. His senses were on high alert, taking in the sounds and smells that drifted on the gentle morning breeze.

Cresta stretched his neck towards the sky, his eyes fixed on a cluster of succulent leaves that dangled temptingly from a high branch. He stretched, but could not reach them. He jumped, and the leaves touched his snapping beak. Despite his best efforts, the prize remained just beyond his reach. Frustrated, he paced back and forth, scanning the area for something, anything, that could aid him. It was then that he spotted it—a sturdy fallen log, half-buried in the underbrush. Cresta nudged the log with his snout, testing its strength, and with a decisive push, rolled it into position beneath the elusive leaves. He climbed atop the makeshift platform, his balance precarious but determined. A few moments later, he triumphantly plucked the leaves from their perch, his ingenuity rewarded.

The flavours of the leaves were vibrant on his tongue—sweet and rich, with a satisfying crunch. Cresta chewed slowly, savouring each mouthful of his hard-earned breakfast. With each bite, his body relaxed. There was something deeply fulfilling about solving a problem, and Cresta basked in the glow of his success, his crest catching the sunlight in a brilliant display of colours.

From his place in the shade, Armor observed the young Corythosaurus with interest. The old Ankylosaur's heavyset form was a stark contrast to Cresta's lithe figure. Armor's back was adorned with bony plates and spikes, a formidable armour against any who might wish him harm. His clubbed tail rested on the ground, leaving small impressions in the soft earth as he shifted his weight. He watched Cresta with a sort of quiet respect, noting the younger dinosaur's resourcefulness. In this world, such cleverness was a valuable trait.

Cresta, having finished his meal, glanced over at Armor and let out a soft hoot, a sound that resonated through his crest. It was a simple acknowledgement, a recognition of Armor's presence. In return, Armor let out a low rumble, a sound that vibrated through the ground and was felt more than heard.

As Cresta stepped off the log and rejoined the world at ground level, the floodplain stretched out before him, vast and teeming with life. The rivers snaked through the landscape, carving paths that would lead to countless adventures.

A little distance away, steam rose from the herd, a soft cloud that mingled with the morning mist. The air was alive with the sounds of the waking world;

distant calls of dinosaurs filled the space between the rustling leaves and the gentle murmur of the river.

The calls of the other dinosaurs echoed in the distance, each one a story waiting to be told. Cresta's journey was just beginning. It was a land of giants and for Cresta and his kin, it was home.

Cresta's keen eyes darted across the lush landscape, the vibrant greens and earthy browns painting a picture of the world he was still learning to navigate. A sudden rustle in the underbrush caught his attention—a small lizard, its scales glistening like tiny jewels, scampered across his path, a flash of life amid the stillness. Cresta's heart skipped a beat, and instinctively, bolted for the safety of the herd's centre. The towering adults, with their watchful eyes and protective stances, offered a haven for the young Corythosaurus. They regarded him with a gentle tolerance, their occasional nudges a silent reminder of his place in the family.

Cresta felt silly. It was just a lizard. He crept back towards the riverside and looked down into the water. Plants, resilient and ever-adapting, clung to the fertile soil, bending to the water's whims. Tiny fish darted through the shallows, their silvery bodies a dance of light and shadow. Insects buzzed and flitted, each a tiny survivor.

He looked across. On the other side of the river, a herd of migrating Chasmosaurus cast long shadows over the ground as they moved in a steady, determined procession. Cresta craned his neck, watching the horned giants navigate the terrain with a grace that belied their size. They followed ancient paths etched into their collective memory and repeated with each turn of the seasons.

The Chasmosaurus' journey lingered in Cresta's mind, they never stopped, never slowed, never rushed.

<u>Cresta</u> grazed on the tender shoots that sprouted at the edges of the water, his body moving in harmony with the others. The herd's life was a complex weave of relationships, each member playing their part. Cresta, young and curious, observed the subtle exchanges of calls and gestures that kept the group bound together. He was but a small thread in the vast network, his bright crest a beacon of his youth, but he was eager to learn. The elders watched him, their wisdom an invisible shield against the uncertainties of the world.

Chapter 2

Cresta stretched his strong legs and ambled towards the freshest greens, dew still clinging to each leaf. Around him, other young hadrosaurs mimicked his movements, their playful nips and shoves painting a scene of carefree youth.

The herd started to slowly move along the riverside, the older ones leading, the young ones like Cresta safely enveloped by the group's protective embrace.

Sagecrest, the elder with a crest worn by time, led the herd with an authority that needed no sound. His scars were a map of survival, each one a story of narrow escapes and battles. Cresta watched him. Maybe one day he would lead. Sagecrest's low, resonant calls cut through the morning air, guiding the herd like a beacon.

Amidst the herd's morning rituals, Echo, a sprightly Lambeosaurus, bounded up to Cresta. Her crest, less pronounced than Cresta's, caught the light as she moved. They greeted each other with a chorus of calls, their crests vibrating with the effort.

Together, Cresta and Echo played. Using their crests to make strange, comical sounds to each other. The other dinosaurs paused, their heads tilting in response to the noise.

The sun climbed higher in the sky, its rays touching the tops of the tall ferns and cycads, casting long shadows across the herd's grazing ground. Cresta, his belly full of the morning's fresh greens, wandered among a patch of low-lying horsetails, only nipping at the tender shoots. The other hadrosaurs, with their broad beaks perfect for stripping leaves, still needed more food. Their massive bodies moved with grace despite their size as they gulped down mouthfuls of leaves until there was nothing left of the horsetail patch.

Sagecrest stepped forward confidently. His deep, resonant call urged them onward, his experience telling him that they would find what they needed elsewhere. The herd trusted in his wisdom, their feet stirring up clouds of dust as they followed. Cresta watched the elder closely, learning from his decisive actions.

Their journey took them through the heart of the floodplain, following the river. Cresta had to dodge suddenly around a Leidyosuchus canadensis basking on the riverbank. It was only just before he blundered into it that he noticed its armoured body still as stone and almost the same colour as the ground in front of him. Nearby, a group of Basilemys turtles dipped in and out of the water, their metre-wide shells glistening like polished stones. The river was a lifeline, supporting a world teeming with creatures great and small.

Finally, Sagecrest halted up ahead, and the herd fanned out into a pasture of red, white and purple flowers. The air was rich with the scent of conifers and the sweet aroma of flowering angiosperms. How he knew to come to this place at this time, Cresta could not imagine, but there was enough food here for the whole herd. They could rest, and play until nightfall.

Chapter 3

The moon cast a pale glow over the floodplain, its light touching the backs of the slumbering herd. But Cresta felt a strange unease. A prickling sensation made his skin twitch. Sagecrest let out a low, rumbling call that seemed to hang heavy in the air. The herd shifted, a wave of movement that passed from one massive body to another. Cresta's heart thumped louder in his chest. Echo, the young Lambeosaurus with the playful spark in her eyes, stayed close to Cresta, her gaze darting into the darkness beyond.

The night wrapped the herd in tranquillity. Stars twinkled above, their light shimmering on the river's surface, but Cresta hugged the soft earth, and listened to the familiar scents of the herd around him. Something was not right. He could feel it.

The gentle hush of the breeze whispered through the leaves, but in the distance, beyond the ridge, the clouds gathered. They were like dark, silent beasts, creeping closer, ready to unleash the fury of the skies. This serene night would be the last before Cresta's world changed forever.

Dawn broke with a menacing growl of thunder, jolting Cresta awake.

The first heavy raindrops pattered against the backs of the sleeping adults. The sky, a mess of angry greys, unleashed a torrent of rain that pelted the earth. Cresta scrambled to his feet, water already pooling around his claws.

The adults were beginning to wake now, heads raising around him to look at the skies. The rain quickly swelled into a drumming cascade that drenched the world in water.

By the time everyone was on their feet, Cresta could see the river rising. He watched as the gentle stream turned wild, the waters churning with a fury that pulled at the roots of ancient trees and sent the smaller creatures scurrying for cover.

The river, once gentle and calm, now roared with an untamed ferocity. It surged over its banks, swallowing trees and carving new paths with reckless abandon. Suddenly, the herd was in motion, a mass of scales and muscle pressing forward, seeking higher ground.

Sagecrest led the way, bellowing as the others did their best to follow, slipping and sliding in the mud and the fallen trees. Cresta, with wide eyes, darted and struggled between them. His legs ached as he fought to keep pace with the others.

The river exploded behind him. A torrent of water rushing down from the mountains spilling out over the plain.

The flood showed no mercy, tearing through the land with a roar that drowned out the calls of the herd.

Cresta, caught in the surge, was swept away from the safety of the group. He felt a surge of panic. His legs, used to the soft earth, now flailed against the relentless push of the floodwaters. He fought to keep his head above the surface, his nostrils flaring as he gasped for air. The world was a blur of rain and rushing water, a cacophony of sound that drowned out all else.

He thrashed in the water, gasping for air, his crest barely visible above the churning waves. The current pulled him downstream, away from everything familiar. Cresta's thoughts blurred with panic, but survival drove him to kick harder, to fight the relentless pull of the water.

In the chaos, Cresta's keen eyes caught sight of a log bobbing in the water. With a burst of effort, he lunged for it, his powerful tail propelling him forward. He scrambled atop the makeshift raft, his claws digging into the bark as the log spun and dipped in the current. Cresta clung on, his body swaying with the motion of the water, his instincts guiding him as he navigated this unexpected challenge.

Around him, the flood was reshaping the landscape, its might touching all in its path. Cresta caught glimpses of other dinosaurs—some clinging to the tops of trees, others not as fortunate, swept away by the relentless surge

He did not know how long he was in the water, turning over and over in the muddy froth. He did not know how far he was carried. Finally, he found purchase on a muddy bank, heaving his drenched body onto solid ground, alone and trembling.

Cresta's breath came in ragged gasps as he surveyed his surroundings. The flood had transformed the land into an unrecognizable maze of water and debris. Trees lay uprooted, their roots exposed like the bones of the earth. The herd was nowhere to be seen, their calls silenced by the storm. Cresta's instincts screamed for him to find them, to return to the comfort of their numbers. But where to start? He shook his crest, water droplets flinging from the tips like tiny crystals, and stared around him.

Chapter 4

He looked out over a transformed world, where uprooted trees lay strewn like the bones of giants and the earth was scarred with new paths carved by the flood.

Cresta stood alone on the elevated patch of earth, his heart pounding in his chest like the drumming of the rain. He lifted his head, his crest catching the first rays of sunlight as the storm clouds began to scatter. With a weak, whimpering call, he reached out for his herd, but the vast silence that followed was a heavy weight on his scales. No answering call, no comforting echo—just the whispers of the wind through the battered foliage. Cresta's gaze swept the horizon. Nothing.

Suddenly, a flurry of movement. A group of half a dozen Ornithomimus picked their way through the debris a few metres away. They had long, graceful legs and slender bodies, covered in blue-green feathers. Cresta watched as they came together and then spread apart, running quickly over the soft mud. They darted this way and that, their sharp eyes scouting for the smallest wriggle of life, their keen eyes searching amongst the scattered remnants of the flood.

Cresta tilted his head slightly as he admired their nimble grace as the flock danced across the mud.

The Ornithomimus sensed Cresta's presence, and for a moment, they paused, their heads turning in unison to face him, asses the threat he might pose. Then, as if by silent agreement, they resumed their search, weaving between the fallen trees and scattered rocks.

Cresta watched the way they communicated with flicks of their tails and subtle shifts in posture. The weight of his own loneliness pressed down on him. His herd was gone. He was alone.

An impulse seized Cresta. He lumbered towards the Ornithomimus, his heavy steps a stark contrast to their light-footedness. They glanced at him, their beady eyes curious. Cresta bent his head and attempted to find something to eat alongside them, but there was nothing there for him. Just the Ornithomimus' insect prey.

Cresta felt clumsy next to their swift sprinting movements, and a few seconds later, they were gone, vanishing into the undergrowth, leaving him alone again.

Cresta knew he could not stay here. He had a choice. He could either head uphill to the highlands that rose behind him or set out back upriver through the flooded lands in the hope of finding his home and his herd again.

The highlands were green and safe from the water, but who knew what predators might live there?

Suddenly, Cresta's ears caught a distant call. It was low, and far off. Was that one of his own kind? He listened. It came from the lowlands, back across the muddy remains of the land. His heart thudded with excitement. He waited but heard nothing more.

He wavered for a moment, then, with the decision made, Cresta cast a lingering glance at the highlands. The safety of the elevated ground might offer a place to hide from the floods, but it was time to leave it behind.

His feet shifted. It was a turning point, a choice that would set the path of his life and maybe his death. His crest's shadow draped over the land as the sun dipped lower, and he began to walk into the mud.

dipped lower, and he began to walk into the mud.

Chapter 5

As Cresta stepped down from the highlands, he entered a world reshaped by the flood's fury. The paths were now a jigsaw of waterlogged earth and debris. Trees uprooted and strewn about, lay like the bones of the earth, exposed and bare. The air was thick with the scent of renewal, a blend of mud and new growth that filled Cresta's nostrils.

The first challenge Cresta faced was a vast stretch of mud that clung to his feet like the hands of the earth, grasping and unyielding. His legs pushed against the muck, each movement a battle of strength and will. He searched for solid footing, his eyes scanning for rocks or fallen branches that might offer firm ground. With a heave of his frame, Cresta found a rhythm, a way to get across the treacherous terrain. His crest bobbed with effort.

As dusk wrapped the world in shadows, Cresta climbed a small rise, leaving the mud slick behind him. His breath came in heavy gusts, misting in the cooling air.

He looked for a place to rest. Darkness brought new dangers. Strange calls, growls, dank, dangerous smells. Cresta curled up in the tangled roots of a fallen tree and tried to rest. The night was filled with the rustling whispers of the dark, but the young Corythosaurus had found a pocket of safety among the muddy roots. His body, dwarfed by the ancient broken tree shrank into the hidden nook.

As the stars began to fade, giving way to the first light of dawn, Cresta's eyes opened.

With the sun rising above the horizon, Cresta emerged from his shelter. The land stretched out before him, a canvas of green, dotted with bursts of colourful flowers that had sprung up in the wake of the flood's retreat. Toothy birds flitted from tree to tree, singing and hunting for insects.

As Cresta navigated the scrubby bushes, a rustling caught his attention. A family of small, furry creatures foraged in the undergrowth, their tiny paws deftly turning over leaves and debris. These mammals, no larger than Cresta's head, were Astroconodon, a common sight in the Cretaceous, and Cresta knew their species well, but he knew something else too. Where there were foragers, there were always hunters. Cresta's instincts told him to be wary; the small creatures were not a threat, but they could attract those who were. With cautious steps, he continued.

Cresta's journey brought him to the edge of the river. Its surface rippled with the reflections of the morning light, and instinct told him he was on the wrong side of it. If he was going to find his herd, he would need to get across. Cresta's eyes traced the water's flow, searching for the narrowest point, the safest crossing.

The river's chill enveloped Cresta as he waded into the current. Water pressed against his legs, urging him downstream, but Cresta fought against it. He leaned into the flow, his tail acting as a rudder, guiding him through the swirling eddies. Each step was a labour, muscles straining and heart pounding. He pushed on, until at last, he emerged on the opposite bank, gasping and triumphant.

Chapter 6

Cresta's heart quickened as his eyes caught sight of the deep impressions in the soft earth. Footprints were faint, but they smelled of home. His kind had been this way.

With renewed energy, he followed the trail, the familiar patterns in the mud gave him hope. The tracks weaved through a stand of ferns, and Cresta followed them deeper into the woodland. He moved with purpose, each step a beat in the rhythm of his quest.

It was darker here. Unfamiliar. The air shifted, carrying a scent that made Cresta's skin prickle. It was the smell of a predator. This was the domain of a hunter.

Cresta froze, his instincts screaming at him to hide. He crept forward, into the cover of thicker bushes, and crouched low. His breath was slow, measured, as he waited for the danger to pass.

Peering from his hiding spot, Cresta saw it as it emerged into a clearing – Gorgosaurus.

Three times his size, and with a head filled with massive teeth, the tyrannosaur stalked slowly, deliberately. The dinosaur's eyes scanned the woodland. It paused, sniffed the air, tasting the scent of its prey.

Cresta watched, silent and still. Suddenly the Gorgosaurus lunged forward. Its jaws sprang open, grabbed at something just out of Cresta's view. The struggle was brief, the outcome certain. Cresta saw a blurred shape, shaken in the jaws. It was an unlucky Astroconodon – little more than a bite for the huge dinosaur. In a few seconds, the Gorgosaurus tipped its head back and swallowed the little mammal whole.

Cresta held his breath. When the Gorgosaurus finally lumbered away, Cresta waited for a few long minutes before he emerged from his refuge, his limbs stiff but unshaken.

The encounter had taught him a lesson. Caution was his shield. He pressed on, each step slow, deliberate and quiet. The Gorgosaurus was still out there, and almost certainly still hungry. With each careful move, he learned to read the land, to understand its secrets and its threats.

The day waned as Cresta found a clearer path, there were more footprints pressed deep into the earth. The familiar smell of his own kind hung in the air, but it was distant, weak. Perhaps he was just smelling what he wanted to smell.

The light of the setting sun painted the world in hues of fire and gold, casting long shadows that stretched out before him. As the darkness crept in,

Cresta became more and more tired, but a Gorgosaurus' territory was wide, and Cresta knew that hunters preferred the night. He only allowed himself to rest when he found himself in a wide, green valley.

Chapter 7

Armor, the Ankylosaur, pushed his way through a dense thicket, his armoured body unharmed by the tangled branches. The flood had tossed him about like a leaf in the wind, and he too was lost. But now he stood firm on the ground. The sun broke through the clouds, casting light on his rugged back. His heavy tail swung slowly from side to side, ready to carve a new path through the chaos.

Armor's eyes, small but keen, scanned the landscape. Trees were scattered, and rivers of mud had carved their way through the land. The scent of wet earth and broken vegetation filled the air. He could recognise none of it.

As Armor squelched through the mud, he heard the soft calls of young dinosaurs nearby. A pair of hadrosaurs, their crests barely formed, and a trio of ceratopsians, still without their full frills, huddled together. Their eyes wide with uncertainty, they watched Armor pass.

As if drawn by an invisible force, they fell in step behind him. Perhaps they sensed safety in his heavy, plated presence. Glances were exchanged, and suddenly a new band had formed, bound together by the need to survive in a world that had shifted beneath their feet. Armor looked back at the little gang following him, swung his head back, and continued through the mud.

Armor moved with purpose, leading his unexpected followers. He chose a path that avoided deep mud and treacherous pits left by the flood. The young ones followed, their steps growing more confident with Armor's every move. They learned to read the signs he followed—the way the water flowed, the direction of the wind. Armur led not with sound or gesture but with his very being, his steady pace providing a silent assurance to the group.

The young dinosaurs began to find their place within the group. The hadrosaurs, nimble and quick, skirted ahead, their eyes alert for danger. The ceratopsians stayed close to Armor's tail, their own small horns a pale echo of the weapons they would one day wield. They communicated with chirps and grunts, the sounds mingling in the air. When Armor stopped to graze, they did too, and when he resumed his march, they followed. Together, they formed a miniature herd amidst the remnants of the flood.

Armor's nose twitched as he sniffed the damp earth, searching for hidden morsels. With a swift movement, he dug into the soft soil, unearthing a cluster of roots. The young dinosaurs watched, their heads tilting in curiosity, and soon they too began to scratch at the ground. Their small claws were not as effective as Armor's, but they managed to find some tender shoots. They learned quickly, copying Armor's technique of pushing aside leaves and digging in spots where the earth was loose. Together, they feasted on whatever the flood had failed to wash away.

The sun climbed higher, warming the land and inviting a pause in the day's efforts. Armor lumbered to a patch of soft ferns, settling his massive body with a sigh that ruffled the foliage. The young ones followed suit, some sprawling out to soak in the sunlight, their scales glistening. Others curled up in the shade, their breathing deep and even in sleep. The air was filled with the gentle sound of rustling leaves and the distant calls of birds. For a brief time, the world seemed at peace.

With an instinctive understanding of the land's new shape, Armor led the way to a clear pond, its surface still as glass. The young dinosaurs trailed behind, their eyes wide at the sight of water. They approached cautiously, sipping the cool liquid while constantly scanning for danger. Nearby, a trio of turtles slid into the pond, disappearing beneath the surface.

The afternoon brought new challenges. A vast mudslide blocked their path, its sticky surface threatening to trap the unwary. Armor, with his wide feet, pressed forward, creating a trail for the others to follow. The ceratopsians, with their heavier front ends, found it harder to move through the mud, but the hadrosaurs danced around the edges, finding firmer ground

As dusk fell, the group settled in a huddle, Armor's bulk forming a protective barrier. The shadows grew long, and the sounds of the night began to rise. The young ones huddled close to Armor, their instincts telling them that safety lay in numbers. Armor remained alert, his senses sharp for any sign of a predator's approach.

Chapter 8

Cresta awoke into a world bursting with greens and browns. It was bright and sunny, and the muddy ground was drying. Tall ferns brushed against his sides, and overhead, the trees reached for the sky. He nibbled on the tender tips of cycads, savouring the fresh taste. His eyes sparkled with each new discovery, his crest bobbing as he moved from plant to plant. Here, a patch of bright berries offered a sweet surprise, while there, the broad leaves of a ginkgo tree provided a crunchy snack. He could no longer smell his own kind on the wind, but he felt he must be heading in the right direction. The landscape was more familiar, and he began to relax.

As Cresta pushed through a thicket, he startled a group of small, scurrying creatures. They chattered in protest, scampering around his feet. These tiny critters, the ancestors of modern mammals, were not used to such large intruders. Cresta watched, fascinated, as they stood their ground, their tiny jaws open in warning. He stepped back, allowing them their space, and they quickly vanished into the underbrush.

Further along, Cresta's attention was caught by a strange, yellow glue oozing from the side of a tree. It hung there, glistening in the sunlight. He poked it with his beak, sniffing. The substance clung to his nose like a sticky glue until Cresta shook his head, flinging the resin away. Not everything is good for eating.

Cresta didn't know it but this resin, the tree's way of protecting itself, would eventually harden into amber trapping seeds, leaves or insects and turning them into fossils.

A rustle in the underbrush drew Cresta's gaze. He approached with caution, his large body moving quietly.

Peering through the leaves, he spotted a lizard, its scales shimmering like tiny jewels. The lizard was still, soaking up the warmth of the sun. Cresta observed from a distance, his breath slow and steady. The lizard, sensing no threat, continued its sunbathing.

Just beyond was a babbling brook. The water was clear, flowing over smooth pebbles and past clusters of reeds. He dipped his snout, drinking deeply, the cool water refreshing him. Fish darted in the shallows, their bodies flashing like quicksilver. Cresta watched them swim while he drank.

Dragonflies zipped over the water, their wings a blur of iridescent blue and green. Further upstream, he noticed a turtle stranded on its back. Cresta approached, careful not to startle the creature. With a gentle nudge of his snout, he righted the turtle, which quickly shuffled off.

T

Chapter 9

Cresta stopped. In front of her, a dip in the ground had been scraped out to form a hollow. Inside, in the soft mud, eight eggs lay. The eggs, large and oblong, were clustered together, their mottled shells a tapestry of earthy colours. Each one was cradled by the earth, arranged with care.

He approached cautiously. Perhaps they belonged to a corythosaurus – one of his own kind. Maybe even one of his herd. They looked freshly laid. The smell would tell him.

Cresta moved closer.

The nest was a marvel, the eggs smooth and surprisingly warm to the touch. Cresta's gaze lingered on the delicate patterns that traced each shell, the lines and speckles.

T

He sniffed. A dark, chilling smell. He knew it at once. Not from the herd, from the forest! A distant roar shattered the silence, rolling through the forest like thunder. Cresta's muscles tensed, a jolt of fear igniting his instincts. Birds took to the sky, a flurry of wings, and smaller creatures scurried for cover.

Caught in a moment of hesitation, Cresta's eyes darted from the nest to the river and back. His heart pounded in his chest. The Gorgosaurus mother exploded through the foliage on the other side of the brook. Cresta's senses were assaulted by her scent, a pungent mix of predator and the wild. It was the smell of a hunter, of death lurking in the shadows.

Cresta felt the ground shake. He turned, his body coiled with tension, and dived away sprinting, without looking back, into the undergrowth.

Cresta's pulse raced as he fled from the Tyrannosaur nest, his feet barely touching the ground. He darted through the underbrush, weaving between the trees. Each breath was a silent gasp. The scent of the predator clung to the air. He felt he could hear her crashing after him, feel her breath on his neck, but he didn't look back. He just ran.

As he put distance between himself and the nest, Cresta's eyes caught the tell-tale signs of the Gorgosaurus' reign over the forest. A path of crushed ferns marked the passage of the massive hunter, and here and there lay the remnants of her feasts, bones picked clean and scattered among the foliage.

A recent struggle had painted the ground in shades of crimson and brown, a carcass lay torn amidst a bed of ferns. Scavengers—a mix of feathered raptors and bold, tiny mammals—darted in and out, claiming their share in hasty gulps. Skirted the carcass without slowing and ran on.

Suddenly, the snap of a twig sent a jolt of adrenaline through Cresta's body. He froze, his eyes locking onto the form of the Gorgosaurus mother, somehow ahead of him now, its snout twitching as it searched for the source of the noise. Cresta became one with the forest, his green and brown hide blending seamlessly into the foliage. The predator's gaze swept over him, a moment stretched into an eternity.

They locked eyes, and suddenly Cresta was running for his life.

Chapter 10

Armor trudged through the dense forest, his heavy footsteps muffled by the thick carpet of fallen leaves. The young dinosaurs followed closely behind. They were hungry, and the usual rustling of the undergrowth, which once promised a feast of insects and small creatures, was eerily silent. Armor paused, his armoured back glinting in the dappled sunlight, as he surveyed the surroundings with a keen eye. The little ones huddled behind him.

The group reached a waterhole, their pace quickening at the promise of refreshment. But the water was muddy, stagnant. The smell was foul. Armor dipped his head, sniffing cautiously at the water's edge before drawing back. They could not drink here. With a low rumble, he turned and moved on.

Chapter 11

Cresta's heart pounded like a drum. The dense underbrush around him seemed to close in, trapping him in a green prison as he sensed the Gorgosaurus closing behind him. He couldn't outrun the creature. His only chance was to be more agile.

He ducked between trees and bushes, swerving this way and that. He felt the ground rising underneath him and zigzagged uphill around boulders and trees.

Behind him, he could hear the Gorgosaurus crashing through the trees. If he could keep climbing, keep to the uneven, sloping terrain, then maybe there was a chance the bigger dinosaur wouldn't be able to follow.

Each breath Cresta took was sharp and quick, his body coiled and leapt ever upwards as the predator's heavy footsteps crunched on the forest floor.

The world narrowed suddenly to the edge of a cliff, the ground falling away into a dizzying drop. Rocks skittered down the slope with the slightest touch, a treacherous path getting thinner and thinner. Cresta's gaze swept the horizon. In front, just the path gave way to a steep drop. Behind him, the predator's growls grew louder. The cliff edge was a cruel trap, one that left Cresta with nowhere to run. He stopped and turned to face the Gorgosaurus.

It was huge. With each step the predator took, the earth seemed to tremble. Its massive form was a dark silhouette against the fading light. Its eyes glinted with a predatory gleam, and its jaws opened slightly, revealing rows of sharp teeth. The predator moved towards him along the thin path. Cresta could feel the heat of its breath as it exhaled, a gust of warm, stinking air.

His mind raced, sifting through the panic for a sliver of hope. He glanced at the rocks underfoot, the cliff beside him, and the encroaching shadow of death. There was a chance, slim as it was, that he could use the cliff's treachery to his advantage. Cresta's muscles tensed, ready to spring into action. His tail swished nervously as he prepared to face the predator head-on.

Cresta's plan was desperate but clear. He eyed the loose stones that littered the cliff's edge. With a surge of adrenaline, he kicked at the rocks, sending them clattering down the slope. The tyrannosaur paused, its attention drawn to the sudden noise. Cresta took his chance, darting to one side as the rocks began to tumble, creating a small landslide. The predator's footing wavered, buying Cresta precious seconds. He leapt with all his might towards and past his attacker, the ground crumbling away beneath him. His feet found purchase on the other side, and he scrambled away. The Gorgosaurus' claws scraped the air just behind him.

Cresta's legs churned beneath him, propelling him forward with all the strength he could muster. Skidding and sliding away down the mountainside. The other dinosaur was too big to follow, too clumsy to turn around on the thin path. Instead, it was forced to back up, slowly along the path, taking care not to fall.

Cresta's desperate flight sent stones skittering down the hillside. The earth grumbled, and a cascade of rocks began to plummet, gathering speed and fury. A cloud of dust rose, cloaking the scene in a thick, choking fog. Behind him, he heard the Gorgosaurus' frustrated bellow.

He had survived.

Cresta's breath came in ragged gasps as he slowed to a stop, his body quivering with exhaustion. The silence that followed the rockslide was deafening. He stood alone, the dust settling around him like a grey shroud. His sides heaved as he gulped down the air, each breath. The adrenaline that had fueled his flight ebbed away, leaving a weary ache in his bones. He was safe for the moment, but the world felt larger and more daunting than ever.

As the dust cleared, Cresta lifted his head. His brush with death had shaken him.

He was now on the sheltered side of the mountain. Down below him, the floodplain spread out. His old territory. The waters were still there in pools, and the land was soggy with mud, and some of the woodlands were scattered with fallen trees, but the river had returned to its old shape. He could see it snaking through the plain. He could see no sign of the herd, but, if they had survived the flood, then somewhere down there, he would find them.

Cresta stood tall on the ridge, his feet feeling the earth's whispers. He raised his colourful crest to the sky, letting out a series of deep, resonant calls. The vibrations travelled through the air like ripples on water.

From somewhere in the distance, a call answered back, a faint, low moan carried by the wind. Cresta's muscles tensed with excitement. He shifted his weight, his gaze locked on the horizon. That distant sound was the call of his herd.

Chapter 12

The descent from the ridge was a cautious affair. The light was failing, and it would have been easy to slip and break a leg. At the foot of the hills, Cresta entered a thin strip of forest, dense with ferns and towering conifers.

As the ground levelled out, Cresta spotted shadows flitting between the trees: a pack of juvenile dromaeosaurs. Their sleek bodies moved with a grace that was both beautiful and terrifying. These young hunters, their eyes sharp, their movements choreographed moved silently, closing in on something. Cresta knew he was not their prey today, but the risk was real. If they saw him alone and unprotected, he would be. He lowered his body, using the foliage as cover, and moved towards the edge of the trees.

He looked out across the plain. Open country. He would be exposed, but he had to risk it. His herd was out there, somewhere beyond the horizon. He had to get to the river.

Cresta peered across the open expanse before him, the grassland stretching like a green sea. He couldn't risk it alone, but there was just a chance. A rumble of footsteps signalled the approach of the Centrosaurus herd. He remembered them from the day before the storm. They made that journey from the river across the plains every day, protected by their numbers, slow and steady. He watched them, a procession of horned faces, trudging grimly through the mud.

As they thundered by, Cresta seized his chance, sprinting out of the cover of the trees and in amongst the Centrosaurus'. Dodging to avoid their feet, Cresta made it through to the other side of the wall of flesh and found himself out on his old home plain at last.

Back in the forest, the young dromeosaurs were closing in on their prey.

Armor with the little dinosaur orphans still tagging along behind, crashed his way noisily towards the plain. Suddenly, they were surrounded. The dromaeosaurs, their eyes glinting stepped out of the undergrowth on all sides.

The little dinosaurs huddled close to Armor and the young predators, curious and bold, edged closer.

Armor simply stopped, turned, swung his hefty tail, the heavy club at its end hurtling through the air, and hit the lead dromeosaur square in the chest. The impact sent it flying into a tree, and it crashed, unconscious to the floor. The other dromaeosaurs scattered, instantly.

Armor turned and continued on with his followers behind him.

From the distance, the faint sound of a Corythosaurus call echoed.

Chapter 13

Cresta's heavy feet pressed into the softening earth as he approached the riverbank. With each step, Cresta uncovered more signs of his herd. A snapped twig here, a flattened patch of grass there. They had been here, and recently. The river was his last obstacle, the only thing between him and the floodplain where he felt sure his herd must still be wandering close by

Fresh shoots of green poked out from the mud, tiny signs of the riverbank's healing. Insects buzzed in the air, and small, scurrying creatures left delicate tracks on the wet soil. Cresta watched as a dragonfly alighted on a new leaf.

Cresta stood at the river's edge and surveyed the river. It still surged with the energy of the rains. This wasn't going to be easy.

Cresta's eyes, bright and alert, scanned the water's surface, judging its speed, its depth.

Suddenly there was a sound. He turned. A bush shook, and out stepped Armor, followed by his band of young followers.

Armor, with his heavy frame and armoured back, stepped up to the river's edge, looked at it uncertainly, and stopped, staring down at his reflection in the flowing water. The river was a challenge, not just for the swift and agile, but for the strong too. Armor's eyes met Cresta's.

With a deep breath that filled his chest, Cresta stepped into the river. The water was cool, a shock against his scaly skin, but he pushed forward. His tail swayed behind him, a rudder steering through the surge. His legs found purchase on the riverbed. He strained against the current. With each determined stride, Cresta pushed forward.

But the river was not to be underestimated. Without warning, a surge of water barreled towards Cresta. Cresta's body tensed, muscles coiling. The surge met Cresta's side, threatening to sweep him away. Yet, Cresta did not falter. He leaned into the wave. He pushed back, his powerful tail, churning the water, his legs digging into the riverbed.

As Cresta battled the river. Armour and the young dinosaurs watched. With each stroke, each push against the relentless water, Cresta moved closer to the far shore, to safety, to his herd. The river roared its protest, but finally, Cresta heaved his body onto the muddy bank, his breaths coming in heavy gasps

Turning back, he saw Armor at the water's edge, the young dinosaurs' eyes fixed on him. With a triumphant call, Cresta encouraged them. Armour, with his armoured shell glistening in the sun, stepped hesitantly into the water. The little ones clambered onto his back, their tiny claws gripping his rough skin. Armour's powerful legs pressed into the riverbed, and he began to move forward, the water swirling around him.

The river swirled angrily against Armor's progress. But the Ankylosaur was a moving fortress, his body a boulder. The little dinosaurs on his back peered over his armoured plates, their eyes wide as they rode across the river.

Cresta watched until at last, the Ankylosaur and his cargo reached the safety of the bank.

Chapter 14

Cresta turned his attention to the sounds that filled the air. And now he could hear them - the calls of his herd were close, a symphony of hoots and honks coming from just out of sight beyond the trees. Cresta set off, his strides long and purposeful, his senses alert. Cresta's crest vibrated with excitement.

As Cresta emerged from a thicket, the herd came into view. They were there, grazing peacefully in the new grass. Cresta bounded forward, his voice joining the chorus of welcomes. Sagecrest, the elder, lifted his head, his wise eyes meeting Cresta's and Cresta took his place beside him.

The herd enveloped him, their bodies full of warmth and safety.

Armor, with the young ones still clinging to him, found a spot at the herd's edge. The little dinosaurs slipped from his back, their excitement palpable as they explored their new sanctuary. The hadrosaurs, with their towering forms and gentle eyes, accepted them without hesitation. The herd, now a patchwork of species, grazed together, a mosaic of prehistoric life under the wide, open sky. Cresta, with his colourful crest and renewed spirit, had found his way back, and the herd was stronger for it.

The once familiar terrain now bore fresh streams and scattered pools, mirroring the sky above. The herd tread carefully, their heavy feet pressing into the soft, damp soil.

Later that day, a challenge arose as the herd approached a swollen stream, its waters too deep for the young to cross. Cresta surveyed the scene, his eyes catching on a bridge of fallen trees, the work of the recent storm. With a confident stride, he led the way, stepping onto the makeshift bridge. The wood creaked beneath his weight but held strong. One by one, the herd followed, their trust in Cresta growing.

Cresta watched the newcomers, the little dinosaurs that had arrived clinging to Armor's back. They were tentative at first, unfamiliar with the giants that surrounded them. But Cresta approached them, his presence reassuring. They nuzzled his flank. He pushed them into the centre of the herd, and as the days passed, they found their place among the hadrosaurs, their playful antics bringing a lightness to the herd's steady rhythm.

Chapter 15

Weeks later, as the sun dipped below the horizon, Cresta and Sagecrest together guided the herd to a lush valley where the floodwaters had deposited rich silt and seeds. The ground was now a tapestry of green, sprouting with fresh shoots and leaves.

The herd's dynamics had subtly shifted since Cresta's return. Sagecrest, with his deep, resonant calls, still commanded respect, but it was Cresta's voice that now stirred the herd into motion. Echo, the young Lambeosaurus, watched Cresta with wide, curious eyes, learning from his every move. Cresta had grown.

Standing at the river's edge, Cresta dipped his head to drink. The water was cool, the ripples reflecting the journey that had brought him here. He saw not just his own reflection, but the echoes of the challenges he had faced. The flood, the predators, the separation from his herd – all had carved him into the Corythosaurus that now stood before the water. As he raised his head, water dripping from his beak, Cresta knew that the journey was far from over. Peace had settled over the herd, and within himself.

Cresta, with each heavy step, chose the path ahead with care. The flood had taught him much; every twist in the river, each bend in the path held a lesson. He led the herd away from the marshy edges where the ground was treacherous, guiding them to where the earth was firm and the grass was plentiful. Cresta paused often, scanning the horizon, his instincts sharpened by the memories of the Gorgosaurus.

Cresta stood on top of a hill, surveying the land that stretched out before him. Cresta's calls mingled with Sagecrest's, a duet that danced on the wind. The elder's deep tones spoke of times long past, while Cresta's vibrant notes sang of the present and the future.

Below him, the hadrosaurs grazed, their silhouettes painted against the fading light. Cresta's crest caught the last of the sun's rays. He turned his gaze to the horizon, to the future, to the adventures that lay ahead. The herd was his family, the land was their home, and together, they would thrive.

THE END.

Cresta's World

About 75 million years ago, in what we now call North America, there was a world unlike anything we see today. This was the time of the Late Cretaceous Period, a chapter in Earth's history where dinosaurs roamed in a world of ancient forests and vast plains.

In this age of giants, the lands were teeming with life. Tall conifers reached for the sky, and ferns covered the ground like a green blanket. It was a time when flowering plants were just beginning to bloom, adding splashes of colour to the landscape.

Our hero, Cresta, was a Corythosaurus, a type of dinosaur known for its striking crest. This crest was not just for show; scientists believe it was used to make sounds, helping Cresta talk to other dinosaurs of his kind. Imagine a world filled with the music of these ancient creatures!

Corythosaurus lived in areas that would become Canada and the United States. Their fossils, including nearly complete skeletons, have been found in places like Dinosaur Provincial Park in Canada. These fossils tell us that adults of Cresta's kind were probably about 30 feet long and walked both on two legs and on all fours.

Cresta's world was a mix of forests and floodplains, where rivers meandered through the land. He ate plants, and with his duck-billed snout, he could snip off leaves and twigs. Scientists think that Corythosaurus might have lived in groups, just like deer or elephants today. Maybe they even looked after their young together!

Then there was Armor, the Ankylosaur. Ankylosaurs were like the tanks of the dinosaur world, covered in bony armour from head to tail. They even had a club at the end of their tail for defence. Imagine a big, slow-moving lizard covered in nature's own shield!

These dinosaurs lived in the same era as Cresta. Their fossils, found in places like Montana, show us their armour and clubbed tails. This armour was their main protection against predators. They, too, were plant-eaters, munching on low-growing vegetation.

But the world of Cresta and Armor wasn't just peaceful forests and rivers. It was also home to fierce predators, like the Gorgosaurus. This dinosaur was a fearsome carnivore, a cousin to the famous Tyrannosaurus rex.

Gorgosaurus was a fast and agile hunter. It walked on two legs and had sharp teeth for catching and eating other dinosaurs. Its fossils, including many complete skeletons, have been found in places like Alberta, Canada. These remains have helped scientists learn a lot about how it lived and hunted.

Another interesting dinosaur in Cresta's world was the Centrosaurus. These dinosaurs had large horns on their noses and frills on their heads. Fossils suggest they lived in large herds. Imagine hundreds of these horned dinosaurs moving together across the plains!

The Centrosaurus probably used their horns and frills not just for defense, but also to show off to each other, much like deer use their antlers today. Their fossils have been found in places like Canada, showing us what their horns and frills looked like.

Cresta's adventure also brings us face-to-face with juvenile Dromaeosaurs. These dinosaurs were smaller and more agile than big predators like Gorgosaurus. They were probably fast runners and could have hunted in packs. Their sharp claws and teeth made them efficient hunters.

The Late Cretaceous was warmer than today, with high sea levels. There were no ice caps at the poles, and the world was full of diverse ecosystems.

The area where Cresta lived was a mix of coastal plains and forests. These forests were filled with different kinds of plants, including conifers, ferns, and early flowering plants. The rivers and floodplains would have been home to a variety of life, from fish to small mammals.

The climate and geography made this a perfect place for dinosaurs to thrive. The variety in plants meant lots of food for plant-eating dinosaurs like Cresta and Armor. And where there are plant-eaters, there are also predators, like Gorgosaurus.

In Cresta's world, the changing seasons would bring different challenges, just like they do for animals today. Sometimes there would be storms and floods, and other times, there might be droughts. These natural events shaped the lives of the dinosaurs and the world they lived in.

So, how do we know all this? Scientists study fossils, which are the remains of living things from long ago. Fossils can be bones, footprints, or even just marks left in mud. By studying these fossils, scientists can piece together what dinosaurs looked like and how they lived.

Some of the best places to find Cretaceous dinosaur fossils are in North America, in places like the Hell Creek Formation in the USA and Dinosaur Provincial Park in Canada. These places are like windows into the past, giving us a glimpse of a world millions of years old.

Cresta's story is not just an adventure; it's a journey through time. It helps us imagine a world that existed long before humans, a world of giants and wonders. And thanks to science, we can learn about and appreciate these incredible creatures and the world they lived in.

Other Animal Stories

ANIMAL STORIES: SEASON 1

T. REX'S BATTLE

A DINOSAUR ADVENTURE BOOK

T.Rex's Battle: Chapter 1

North America. 68 Million Years Ago...

In the heart of a dense, cretaceous forest, the early morning light crept through the towering ferns and ancient trees. The air was fresh and filled with the sounds of a world waking up. Deep within this lush world, under a canopy of green, lay a huge nest. It was a large, circular structure, two metres in diameter, a ring of mud scraped up into a protective ring and filled with branches. It sat in a shallow depression in the earth, carefully chosen for its concealment and protection.

At the centre of the nest were two enormous eggs, each the size of a large watermelon. Their surfaces were rough, with a texture resembling cracked leather, and speckled with shades of brown and green. The shells were thick – thick enough to protect the precious life growing inside, strong enough to withstand the weight of a watchful parent but today, they would break.

The area around the nest was trampled down, the signs of a massive creature's regular visits evident in the deep, heavy footprints imprinted into the soil. These tracks painted a clear picture of the diligent care the mother took of her nest.

Around the perimeter of the nest, the detritus of the forest lay scattered - broken branches, fallen leaves, and the occasional feather from a passing bird. This debris added another layer of disguise, blending the nest into the forest floor's mosaic of life and decay.

One of these eggs began to shake. Tiny cracks appeared on its surface, spreading like a spider's web. Inside, something pushed against the hard shell. With a final effort, a small snout broke through, gasping for its first breath of cool, damp air.

Tara the Tyrannosaurus Rex lay still for a moment, her newly opened eyes adjusting to the dim light filtering through the dense foliage.

She wriggled, pushing more of her body out of the egg. Her tiny arms, already strong, clawed at the edges, tearing the shell apart. She tumbled out onto the soft nest, a ball of damp feathers and heaving breaths.

Tara was small, roughly the size of a turkey. Her body, though tiny in comparison to the adult she would grow into, was robust and well-proportioned, with sturdy legs that suggested power and speed. Covering Tara's skin was a fine coat of fluffy feathers which were a mottled blend of earthy browns and soft greens. They camouflaged her almost perfectly against the forest floor.

She raised her large, heavy head and looked around with curious eyes that glimmered. Her snout sniffed the air, and she opened her mouth and yawned. Rows of tiny, sharp teeth glittered in the sun.

The forest was a blur of colours to Tara's new eyes. Green leaves waved above, and the sunlight cast dappled patterns on the ground. Slowly things came into focus.

Around her, the forest was alive. Tiny lizards skittered in the underbrush, and high above, pterosaurs soared between the gaps in the canopy.

The distant roar of larger dinosaurs echoed.

Nearby, the other egg rocked and trembled as another young T. rex prepared to emerge.

With unsteady legs, Tara rose. Her movements were clumsy. The world around her was vast, a maze of towering ferns and wide, ancient trunks. She stumbled, her tail swaying to balance her small, hefty body.

A shadow passed over the nest, and from nowhere, there was her mother, a towering figure, looming over her.

Tara's eyes struggled to focus on the huge shape. The massive head turned towards the nest, her eyes observing her baby. She let out a low, rumbling sound which shook the earth.

The air was filled with the scents of the forest: the earthy aroma of damp soil, the fresh scent of leaves, and something else – a hint of something wild and untamed. Tara sniffed the air.

Hunger gnawed at her belly. She had never eaten before, but instinct told her she needed food. The forest around her teemed with life, small creatures that scurried and buzzed. A part of her wanted to struggle out of the nest and chase them, but she didn't know why.

Her mother stepped closer, her massive feet thudding softly on the forest floor. In her mouth, she carried a prize: a chunk of meat. It was soft and red. She carefully laid it down in the nest, and Tara's eyes widened. It smelled hot and thick.

She staggered towards it, sniffed it, and then opened her mouth and sank her teeth into the raw flesh, wrenching it back and forth to tear a piece off, then swallowing it whole. The taste was powerful and salty.

Behind her another hatchling, was freeing itself from its shell. Tarok's egg rocked back and forth. His legs kicked, sending cracks racing across the surface. Finally, with a small grunt, he broke free, his small body tumbling into the nest beside his sister.

Tarok blinked, his eyes wide as the sounds of rustling leaves and distant calls filled his ears. Their mother loomed over them, her massive form protective and warm. She lowered her head, her nose gently touching each hatchling in turn. They responded, pressing their tiny noses back against her, the comforting scent of their mother filling their senses.

Tarak spotted the food, and dived at it, grabbing a chunk of his own. The two siblings were a flurry of movement and noise, jostling each other for the best scraps. Tara pushed her way through, her tiny jaws snapping instinctively at her brother.

The meal was a frenzy, each hatchling tearing at the flesh, driven by hunger and instinct. Tara bit and clawed, tasting the meat, and feeling the strength it gave her. She gulped down mouthful after mouthful until there was nothing left in the nest but feathers and bits of shell still clinging to their wet bodies.

After their meal, their mother pushed the baby dinosaurs to the edge of the nest, nudging them with her nose.

Tara was first out into the world. The forest floor was a patchwork of light and shadow, filled with strange and wondrous things.

The two wandered in the small clearing. Tara found a pool of water, its surface calm and reflective. She peered into it, seeing her own reflection for the first time. She cocked her head, watching as the tiny reflection did the same. Then, with a splash, she stepped into the pool, sending ripples across its surface. The cool water felt good against her skin, washing away the remnants of the egg and her first meal.

Tara's legs were still shaky. Her head felt heavy, but she managed to push it up, her eyes level with the towering ferns that surrounded the nest. Tarok was unsteady too, his tail swinging to balance as he took his first wobbly steps outside the nest. Their mother watched, a silent guardian as they explored the edges of their clearing.

For the first few days of their lives, Tara and Tarok played in the clearing. Tara leapt onto a pile of leaves, pretending it was a small creature she had caught. Tarok crept through the underbrush, his eyes fixed on his sister, learning how to move quietly, how to surprise.

Tara chased a lizard. It was fast, but she was faster. She learned to predict where it would dart next. Tarok snapped at flying insects, each catch sharpening his reactions. With each attempt, they grew more skilled and more confident.

As night fell, the hatchlings would return to the nest, under the protective gaze of their mother. They would curl up beside her, her warmth a promise of safety. In the shelter of the ancient forest,

Tara and Tarok fell into a deep sleep.

Now read on...

Printed in Great Britain
by Amazon